06-24-17

To Adaida

The Beauty of Love

SO-BAU-068

Yours Watching

The Beauty of Love

Selected Poems

Doris Washington

Book Cover & Photographs by Joni Meyers
Author Photograph is supplied by the Author

Copyright © 2015 by Doris Washington.

Library of Congress Control Number: 2015903281
ISBN: Hardcover   978-1-5035-4861-9
           Softcover   978-1-5035-4862-6
           eBook   978-1-5035-4863-3

Print information available on the last page.

Rev. date: 03/20/2015

To order additional copies of this book, contact:
Xlibris
1-888-795-4274
www.Xlibris.com
Orders@Xlibris.com
707484

Contents

Dedication

I dedicate this book to my dearest and loving husband John,
Whose love and support has made this work all possible,
And to my son John, who has been my inspiration to write.

Acknowledgements

I would like to give special thanks to my mother Emma Buchanan, my brothers and sisters, For their love and support. And also, I would like to give special thanks to my dear friends, Barbara Roopnaraine, Audrey Edwards, Marilyn Donley, Afi Roberson, Priscilla Gallegos, Joni Meyers and to those special friends for through their belief in me, their encouragement and support has helped make this book possible to create.

Reflections, My Personal Story Living with Autism

Over 22 years ago, on December 27, 1993, a traumatic incident that involved my son who has autism with two police officers, greatly impacted my life. My son who was 18 -years -old at the time was playing outside his front yard, when two police officers not aware of his autism held him on the ground with handcuffs. My son had suffered a separated shoulder as a result of the incident. I filed a lawsuit against the two police officers and settled the case in 1998. My son's case led to a Statewide Training Program *Recognizing Special Needs* that was implemented in 2001 in Pennsylvania. Shortly after my son's incident my writing began. My hope is that police officers across the nation will implement a training program to be aware of and recognize persons with special needs, so that incidents such as my son's will be a thing of the past.

I share poems about inner peace, holding on to faith each day in the course of our daily lives, hope, healing, autism awareness, inspiration, God's Peace, and love. As I travel across the country to numerous of book signings, I help bring the awareness of autism by sharing my personal story living with autism, in bringing the importance about the incident that occurred in December 1993.

His Window

As he looked in his window – that one cloudy day.
Two men of service and authority proceeded to come his way.

One was in plain clothes and the other in uniform of blue.
They didn't know he had a disability -neither men had a clue.

They didn't notice certain characteristics that he had-
Autism! -you know.
For if they knew-
They would have proceeded to go slow.

His scream echoed and his mother ran outside-
He was held on the ground, handcuffed and not free.
And as she watched thinking *"How could this be?"*

As she looked in her son's face- his eyes cried out of his pain.
She continued watching in awe-
Her son lay helpless,
She quietly cries for him- her tears are like rain.

As her son is held on the ground-
She tells them: *"This is my son."-*
A child of her own.
One of them questions her: *"Is this your home?"*

They release him,
He goes in the house,
And she's still outside talking to them
On that cloudy day.
It was not too long before they proceeded to go their way.

She tells them her son has autism,
As she hurts for him that day.
They could not understand the error of this-
And they go their way.

His shoulder is separated.
His mother cries out.
She does not know what to do.

He Hurts!
She Hurts!
So Much Pain!-
Both mother and son are – *Blue.*

Some years have passed-
Since that cloudy winter day-
As mother and son start anew.

For he still thinks of that cloudy day-
When he looked in *his window*
Don't you see?
On that cloudy day in *December 1993.*

When December Comes

When December Comes-
He is not the same.
Memories of that cold winter day-
Are with him – *Again and Again.*

When December Comes –
He thinks about what happened to him.
As he played outside and they approached him.

When December Comes-
He remembers the *hurt and pain-*
He went through.
Years have come and gone,
And a little part of him is – *Blue.*

When December Comes-
He goes through it,
Adjusting – but not ok.
For his life has changed because of it.
And with him it- *stays.*
When December Comes

The Storms

He didn't promise they'll always be days of sunshine.
For rainy days do come,
And sometimes they may seem
To last forever.

Believe He will always be there
To get you through any storm,
Yes! – any storm imaginable.

Sometimes storms may be a test of one's faith.
For as you trust in Him-
To know with no doubt
All will be alright- no matter how heavy the storm.

He will carry you when you cannot carry yourself.
He will bring you through
Even if it seems hopeless.
Know that He is *hope* to hold to.

He didn't promise they'll always be days of sunshine.
But He did promise
He will always be there through it all.
For He will bring a *Blessing* through-
The Storms!

Foreword

The Beauty of Love are a selection of poems that express inner peace, positive thinking, encouragement, faith, hope, healing, autism awareness, inspiration and love. In each chapter of poems, I write an inspiring message of what each chapter is about. In this selection, I have combined new poems with familiar poems as a continuing saga to touch the hearts of many readers all over the world.

We can all relate through the course of our daily lives, that life is forever changing. And we can always use words of inspiration through the challenges of life. In this selection, readers will find throughout the entire book, many poems that touch the heart with inspiration. Also in this selection, are three poems *His Window/ When December Comes/ The Storms,* which I dedicate for autism awareness. These three poems are in the section following *Reflections, My Personal Story Living with Autism.*

In my poems *Hold on to the Sunshine after the Rain* and *The Storms,* I express how to have faith through the difficult times of one's life, and to believe that God will see you through.

For today may not be your tomorrow. In my poems *Take Me to Your Place* and *The Beauty of Love,* I express that one finds inner peace by seeing the positive side in every situation. Also in this selection, I share poems that I have written in honor of those unique individuals that I admire in making a difference, *A Soldier for Peace* in honor of Dr. Martin Luther King Jr, *A Pioneer's Journey* in honor of Coretta Scott King, and *This Day, A Dream, A Promise Fulfilled,* in honor of

President Barack Obama. And in the poem *The Way of Love,* I share that when we go with love, we invite others to know love.

I wanted to give readers all over poems of inspiration that are my favorites, along with a variety of new poems that I have written that we all can relate to. That no matter your walk through life, we all share one thing in common. That there will be storms. And to get through those storms, we need a spirit of inspiration that will see us through. My greatest hope is that *The Beauty of Love* will help provide the inspiration that we so need in our daily lives today.

As Tomorrow Comes

God did not promise us that there will always be days of sunshine. What He did promise, He will always be there through the sunshine and through the rain. Storms do come, and they may seem to last forever.

But as one trust in Him to know that no matter how heavy the storm may be, storms doesn't last forever. Sometimes the rain comes to make room for the sun to shine even brighter. For today may not be your tomorrow.

Hold On To The Sunshine After The Rain

We can see the sunshine after the rain.
And no matter how difficult
The storm,
It will be alright.

We can find strength for each day-
As we hold on to *His Promise*-
For He'll carry us through
With *His Mercy- His Love* so dear.

We can see the light through the darkness.
And believe with the astounding *faith*-
That He'll always be there- *Always*.

We can rise above any storm imaginable-
For with Him all things are possible.
Yes! All things are possible with- *Hope*.
And we can see the sunshine-
After The Rain.

Hope

Giving up is surrender to no place.
When all seems lost, holding on
Brings you one step closer to the promise.
And as you believe each day is a new day,
Your trials can be your triumph.
Just believe that it all gets better,
No matter your circumstance,
No matter what you go through.
Believe what is now can change tomorrow.
Believe with Faith.
And always hold on to-
Hope.

As You're Going Through

I can worry when things aren't what
They should be.
I can be stressed every minute,
Every hour of the day when problems arise.

I can feel my heart with anxiety when it seems
It's not getting better.
I can take my stress level to another level,
Angry, bitter and just feeling not so good at all.
Yet, I can see the sunshine through it all.
He's taught me that so very much.
And as I believe tomorrow will be better
Than I can ever imagine-
I'm at Peace.

The Sunshine

When your day seems cloudy and gray.
Pray the Lord will take your blues away.
Just Look for the Sunshine

And before you know it, what's troubling you.
Will start to go away, and you're no longer blue.
Just Look for the Sunshine

For you decide how you live for whatever way
You choose.
And if your way of living is positive,
You have nothing to lose.
Just Look for the Sunshine

For if you wear a smile and not a frown.
You'll find many of life's challenges will not get you down.
Just Look for the Sunshine

Remember to keep the love in your heart.
For staying positive is the most important part.
Just Look For-
The Sunshine!

My Prayer For You

I pray His Love will shower upon you each day.
May His arms surround you,
To encourage you through your travels,
To comfort you when you need a friend,
To guide and sustain you through the most
Difficult times.

May you find joy as the morning comes.
And may it stay with you as the sun goes down,
To hold you to the new day at the break of dawn.

I pray His Love shower upon you each day
Of your life.
May His Love be with you always.

God's Peace

When the world seems too much to bear,
Too much to grasp,
I seek your peace within.
I find your strength to sustain me at all times.
And I pray more than ever before.
For it's your peace that flows like
The water along any brook or stream.
It's your peace that makes the new fallen snow
So beautiful on a brisk winter's morning.
It's your peace when the birds sing so lovely
On a warm summer's day.
It's your peace when the leaves fall
So gently in October.
It's your peace so beautiful.
When the world seems too much to bear,
Too much to grasp-
I look up to know you're always there.
With you-
Such Peace-
I Find.

The Storms

He didn't promise they'll always be days of sunshine.
For rainy days do come.
And sometimes they may seem to last forever.

Believe He will always be there
To get you through any storm.
Yes! – any storm imaginable.

Sometimes storms may be attest of one's faith.
For as you trust in Him-
To know with no doubt
All will be alright-no matter how heavy the storm.

He will carry you when you cannot carry yourself.
He will bring you through.
Even if it seems hopeless.
Know that He is *hope* to hold on to.

He didn't promise they'll always be days of sunshine.
But He did promise
He will always be there through it all.
For He will bring a *Blessing* through –
The Storms.

As Tomorrow Comes

Hope may seem difficult to hold on to.
And whatever challenges you may
Experience at the present day,
Know it's a temporary thing.
For today may not be your tomorrow.

Hold on to *Hope* when it seems
Difficult to do so.
Just Hold On.
And believe the sun will rise again.
Yes!
The sun will rise-
As Tomorrow Comes.

The Joy In The Morning

Life has its storms.
And there's always the joy in the morning
That can carry you through the night,
And the next day after that.
When problems arise,
And there seems no relief.
Hold on to the joy.
Let the sun shine though.
Believe it all takes care of itself,
No matter the storm.
And you'll find peace.
For Life has its Storms.
And there's always –
The Joy In The Morning!

Thank You For This Day

Live life with a song in your heart. Be thankful for each day you so awake. Take each moment as if it's your last. For every day we so have is precious. Life is full of joys and challenges. But as we seize the moments of joy, and rise above the challenges, we may find life itself is a blessing.

Blessings are what He so gives to us each day. And life can be a joyful song to sing. Always live life with a song in your heart. For with a joyful song to sing, You will always be blessed.

Thank You Forever More

On this winter night-
As I close my eyes-
Before I lay down to sleep.
I just want to Thank You.
Thank You forever more.

For no matter my joys- my trials -
Your mercy – Your love is so amazing.
I just want to Thank You-
Thank You forever more.

And for each day I awake
To see the morning sun.
I hold on to- *a blessing* –
A prayer answered.
I just want to Thank You-
Thank You forever more.

On this winter night-
As I close my eyes-
Before I lay down to sleep.
Dear Lord!-
I just want to Thank You.
Thank You Forever More!

This Day Today

This day today,
I took a moment to breathe,
To laugh,
And to smile.

This day today,
I saw hope through the disappointments.
To stay always encouraged.

This day today,
I focused on the goodness.
To know all gets better if one believes.

This day today,
I practiced the act of Faith,
To keep going,
To never give up.

This day today,
I took a moment to breathe,
To laugh,
To smile,
And to Pray!
This Day Today!

Friends I Know

Fondly I say there are those friends I know-
Whose love is so wonderful to have in one's Life.
Those little things that we sometimes take
For granted, those friends I know- Do!

When those friends I know call me to see if I'm ok.
When those friends I know encourage me to
Never give up.

When those friends I know make me laugh
Through the sunshine,
And through the rain.
When those friends I know always have a listening ear.

When those friends I know don't mind my imperfections,
Just love me as I am.
When those friends I know take the time to get to know me-
Just to know me.

When those friends I know care,
And offer support and love.
Yes! I'm so glad I have in my life-
Those-
Friends I Know!

I Have A Song In My Heart

I hear the birds Sing.
I receive the Lord's Blessing.
Oh! How beautiful the Sound.
God's presence is all around.

I sing no sad song.
Unhappiness does not last long.
With such joyful tears,
I've learned through the years.

Life is precious and worth living.
The best of me I keep giving.
I trust in God always.
Peace,
Joy,
And Love I carry with me
The rest of my days.
For-
I Have A Song In My Heart!

Clouds For Today

The clouds tell us where we're going,
And the rain which is constant relays
So much.
Will the sun come-
Oh Yes!
It will tomorrow.
Spring doesn't seem like spring
At this moment.
The seasons will change a bit.
For all this has been foretold.
But will the sun shine.
Oh Yes!-
It will tomorrow.
Know this will pass.
Yes, It will.
The clouds don't have to cloud
Our hearts.
And the rain doesn't have to
Make us blue.
Remember the sun can shine,
Even when you don't see it.
The sun can shine in- *you!*
For right now, there are just-
Clouds For Today.

Morning

Yesterday has come and gone.
Tomorrow brings promise,
And always hope.
And for now,
I'm doing alright.
Yes! I'm doing just fine.
And each breath I take-
It's Good!
Yes! –
It's All Good!
Hello-
Morning!

Avenues

Alone I walk in the morning sun.
I find there're many roads to venture to.
Not sure where I'm going,
For there're many directions
To follow through.

With so much before me,
I find things can change
From one minute to the next.
And I'm learning life
Is all about passing the test.

I ask the Lord to be my teacher.
I ask the Lord to be my guide.
And no matter what my life may be-
I feel His Love inside.

Alone I walk in the morning sun,
I find there're many roads to venture to.
Not sure where I'm going,
For there're many directions
To follow through.
There Are Many-
Avenues.

Thank You For This Day

Dear Lord-
I thank you for this day.
This day as I begin a new found journey.
Full of the promise and the faith I have found
With You!
I thank you for each blessing you bestow upon me.
I sing with abounding joy of your love.
And as I awake each day,
I ask for your anointing –
Giving me the reassurance
That with-
Your grace,
Your mercy,
I can always begin again.
Dear Lord-
I Thank You For This Day.

I Wish To Live Life

I want to receive the Lord's Blessings every day.
I want to be at my best,
Even if I'm at my worst in every way.

I want to hold on to only good feelings in my heart.
I want to move on from disappointments
As I make a new start.

I want to be receptive of change and not lose me.
I want to always in every situation,
Open my eyes and see.

I want to look back at the past to reflect,
And not feel sorrow.
I want to hold on to hope
As I look forward to tomorrow.

I want to always to *"keep the faith"*
For dreams to come true.
I want to not remain sad, lonely, and blue.

I want to always let positive thinking
In my life play a vital part.
And-
I want to always have *Love* in my heart.
For-
I Wish To Live Life!

Take Me To Your Place

We long for that inner peace in our daily lives. And to let go is not an easy thing to do. But as we start to let go of things we cannot change, we'll find such peace within. To look at your heart in how you may be perceiving any given situation is a beautiful place to be.

Sometimes when we think that we are so right about someone or any situation, that on the surface seems to be true, most of the times is not. The important thing is to look at your thoughts with a positive attitude, and always with love. For as you let go and let love take you, you'll find that with acceptance comes peace.

The Morning Sun

Revelations came to me
At the break of dawn.
Realizing many things.
Looking over my life,
How it has been,
Where I am now,
And where I am going.
Letting go of issues from others,
Issues I have, I'm facing
What I can't change.
And I'm moving forward to a new change.
My healing begins.
And I can see clear,
As I see-
The Morning Sun

The Wilderness

Darkness surrounded me, I could not find the light.
The Light was there, but I could not see it.
Assumptions of what I perceived became my reality.
Negative energy kept coming in when I least expected.

Loneliness,
Bitterness,
And despair engulfed my spirit,
I could not breathe.
Then a voice said: *"Come With Me."*
He talked to me there.
He guided me to a place of peacefulness that I've never known.
There were many trees to guide me along the way.

They were marked with directions to where
I was meant to be.
I then began to see the light through the darkness.
The Blessings that were always there,
I began to see and receive.

His Love filled me.
His Love engulfed me.
Positive thoughts became my reality.
I was no longer misguided.
The place I was meant to be was not far.
With Him I was not alone.
For with His Light, He saw me through-
The Wilderness.

Letting Go

Cleansing in one's soul.
Peace,
And serenity flows.
Hurt,
And pain released.
Your heart at peace.
Love steps in,
As you surrender it to Him.
Letting Go!

Familiar

As I travel on this Journey of mine.
There're many doors to open,
And I'm confronted
With a place I once knew.
Knowing I can't go back.
For there're things I must do.

In order for me to grow,
What was,
I must move on,
And let go.
And as I open many doors I see
The places where I need to be.
Leaving what is-
Familiar

Start Over

There comes a time when one must make a change,
And move on.
For there're things you cannot change,
And if you are hurting,
Don't let it last too long.

And if holding on to things causes you pain,
It's best to let go.
For letting go is best for one's soul.

Look forward to new beginnings,
And don't look back.
Keep your spirits high,
Even when you feel at your
Lowest, for you'll stay on track.

Hold on to hope and promise as you start each day.
And you'll find many Blessings-
Beautiful in every way.
For You Can Always-
Start Over.

Whirlwind

In a whirlwind spinning
Out of control.
Finally stepping back
To see what direction
You're taking.
Is it good?
Is it right?
Understanding what is meant to be.
Revaluating all of it since it started,
And where it is now.
Then to realize for self,
That Acceptance is Peace.

Perspective

It's all in the attitude how you see any situation.
It's all in your perspective.
Sometimes we see what we want to see
That may not always be the truth.
Sometimes we need to step back and hear
What we did not hear, to hear it again.
And sometimes we just need to let go,
Even when we feel we're right.
One's attitude can change a course
Of one's direction in life.
And a positive attitude can take you to
Beautiful places that you could never dreamed possible.
Remember one can change their destiny.
It's all in the attitude.
It's all in your-
Perspective.

Take Me To Your Place

Touch me My Father!
Shower me with your
Goodness and grace.
Help me stay still in times of trouble,
And for whatever trials I may face.
Take Me to Your Place

Strengthen me in the Spirit,
So your voice is the only voice I hear.
Stay with me, and talk to me,
Whether it be far or near.
Take Me to Your Place

Anoint me!
Lift me up in your spirit.
Help me accept and love others for
Who they are.
Grant me everlasting peace.
And if I stray Lord too far! -
Take Me To Your Place!

Peace

Sometimes forgiving can be difficult,
Especially when feeling hurt and disappointed.
Sometimes even when the world is unkind,
Being right doesn't hold too much.
Letting go can be such a wonderful feeling,
And the world will seem much nicer.
It's a matter of perspective.
It's a matter how to deal with it
In your mind- in your heart- in your soul.
To let go with no hesitation for the simple
Reason to be at-
Peace.

A Journey Of
A Thousand Steps

Never give up on your dreams. Believe in the deepest desires of your heart that all is possible. Sometimes life can bring you a curve. Sometimes life can bring many challenges. And sometimes there are bumps in the road.

It doesn't matter how long the journey, what matters you go the distance all the way to the end. He always has a design for where you are to be at every given moment. And sometimes it's the disappointments where He test your faith even more. Always stay encouraged through every situation.

Follow your dreams. For one single step leads to a thousand steps making dreams come true. What may seem impossible is possible when you believe.

Courage

Don't be afraid to step out on faith?
Have the courage to fulfill your dreams.
For it's *your faith* that steers you forward
To face any obstacle along the way.

Life is full of challenges each and every day.
And all that you hope to achieve isn't always easy.
But as you keep going and believe in your passion.
He will take you to places you wouldn't thought possible.

For endurance is the strength He gives to you.
To know what you dream to be will come to be.
For as you believe, you'll find true success and
Fulfillment will be yours.

Don't be afraid to step out on faith?
Have the courage to fulfill your dreams.
For dreams do come true-
Always with one's –
Faith.

True Beauty

The *true beauty* is always inside of you.
That inner spirit that we all have.
To like who you are.
To find your own gift.
And discover your own uniqueness.

Know that you are already beautiful
With what He has given only to you.
For we all have *a purpose -*
A *passion* to fulfill in this life.

And we all have a choice to live our dreams-
To give the best of ourselves-
Our gift to the world.

For as you start to see the *true beauty*
That is inside of you.
You'll be able to let others see it too.
For the *True Beauty* is always –
Yes Always! –
Inside of – you.

I Cannot Stay Where I Am

This change I find in me,
Empowers me to never give up.
To endure,
With Faith.
And whatever obstacles along the way,
I can overcome.
Today I own this for self,
And go forward with a new vision
To know all things I dream for,
Hope for,
I can achieve.
I cannot stay where I am.
And I Thank You Lord For This.

Road Blocks

As I keep going each day.
I am finding many Road Blocks along the way.

Whether I go left or right.
Going forward- traveling day or night.

The Road Blocks are always there.
Feeling helpless and in despair.

Frustrated!
Not knowing what to do.
I remember that Prayer is the answer,
And I come to know the Lord
Will see me through.

And as I journey on- I continue on with the
Many Road Blocks along the way.
And again, I remember to Pray.

For the Lord is never forsaking.
He gives me strength,
And I stay strong.
And as He sees me through- I continue on.
For there are many-
Road Blocks

Alone

Alone does not always stand for lonely.
Sometimes it's a great healing- that space
To grow.

Alone sometimes helps you with a great
Sense of focus and perspective.
And the trials can be triumphs.

Alone sometimes helps you stay encouraged,
Empowering you to many heights- many possibilities.

Alone is a period each of us experiences for however
Long it may be.
Overcoming barriers -moving forward with belief
In one's self.

Alone does not always stand for lonely,
For it can take you to other places, expanding
Your horizons,
And finding you're not-
Alone.

The Comfort Zone

Great achievements does not come easy.
Sometimes you have to venture out
Of the Comfort Zone.

The journey may seem long,
And you may wonder the dreams you set
Will come to surface.

Oh! The comfort zone where all is good
And comfortable-
Why should one leave chasing rainbows?

But that's the joy of it all.
Visualizing your dreams to come true.
Visualizing what you can achieve,
If you only believe,
And keep going with the persistence,
And faith.
Your dreams can come true.
Leaving-
The Comfort Zone

Make Your Dreams Come True

Fly high little *blue bird-*
Fly high above the sky.
Go beyond the horizons-
Always continue to try.

Don't let others opinions discourage
Or limit you.
Always keep your spirits high,
No matter what you go through.

Stay the course,
Even when the going is rough.
Be persistent,
Keep going,
And never give up.

And when others say you cannot-
You say you can.
Find your own uniqueness,
And remember you are your best friend.

And most of all believe in yourself,
Never stop believing in you.
So fly high little *Blue Bird-*
Make Your Dreams Come True.

A Journey Of A Thousand Steps

You must never give up when it seems so far.
You must never doubt when it all seems it's going nowhere.
You must never say you can't-always say you can.
It doesn't matter how long the journey.
What matters that you give it your all,
All the way to the end.
A true winner never gives up,
Never doubts when things go wrong.
Always gearing with positive energy,
No matter how the road turns.
For one single step leads to a thousand steps,
Making dreams come true.

Winners

Winners see beyond the boundaries,
Always searching high.
Winners always say: *"I can do it."*
Believing their dreams can come true.
Winners never quit.
They stay the distance all through the end.
Winners don't compare themselves to others.
Only strive for the best in themselves.
Winners live by courage and faith.
Standing tall with a job well done.
Winners see beyond the boundaries,
Always searching high.
Shining beautiful like a Star!

Always There

Healing begins through forgiveness. Your hurt and pain is washed away. And no matter about yesterday's sorrows, one can go on with a renewed faith. You always have a choice to change your life. Believe that He can change your life around. And what is so amazing about His Love, is that He always gives you a second chance- a third chance - a fourth chance.

Sometimes the trials in life can be most difficult to bear. But as you trust in Him to know that He will work it all out in time. For with Him, life will be brighter than you can ever have known. You can always begin again.

The Love Inside Of You

Take the disappointments
And make them your blessings.
Always stay positive no matter
What each day brings.

For it's all up to you.
You always have a choice
To live a full or half full life.

Rise above what you cannot change.
And focus on what you can.
For yesterday is past,
And today is a new day.

There's always a blessing through
Every experience.
And with each experience –
There's always something you can learn.

Live each day as if it's your last.
Press forward with faith.
And most importantly –
Always Keep-
The Love Inside of You.

A New Day

I awake from a long sleep,
Yes a long sleep from loneliness,
Self pity,
And regret.
I no longer choose to taste the bitter tongue
Of the trials of life.

I no longer allow worry, self-doubt,
And negative energy to be the focus of existence.
I no longer starve for others approval,
Opinions and love.

Forgiveness is what I practice.
Patience has become my daily routine.
Love keeps me alive.
And I seek Him always.
As I Start-
A New Day

I Can Always Begin Again

My healing begins through forgiveness.
My hurt- my pain is washed away.
And as I find the *love*
Always inside of me-
I can begin again.
I can start anew.

He may close a door-
For another door to open.
And life's twist and turns
May be too much to bear at times.
But as I lean on Him-
Trust in Him to know
He'll work it all out in time-
Oh! Such peace I find.

And with that I can see a new day
Always starts with me.
To understand what I cannot change
I must surrender it all to –Him.

My healing begins through forgiveness.
My hurt- my pain is washed away.
And as I fill my heart with His Love-
I Can Always Begin Again.

Accepting

Healing from the hurt and pain.
I cry no tears like rain.
I Am- Accepting

Letting go of things that don't change.
Cleaning out the junk in my heart-
Only to rearrange.
I Am- Accepting

To Rearrange! To Rearrange!
Putting things in priority.
Seeing Blessings, and no excess baggage I carry.
I Am- Accepting

Moving away from disappointments.
Picking up the broken pieces to begin again.
Never giving up on life.
Loving who I am.
Believing I am my best friend.
I Am- Accepting

Not wearing a frown.
Carrying only a smile.
Giving my worries to God.
And all the while.
I Am-
Accepting

Start Anew

When you start anew,
Just remember to keep you.
For each situation you journey is different.
And each one you meet is not the same.
Go into each experience leaving issues
Of the heart behind.
Let positive thoughts fill your mind.
Forgive, even if it's hard to do.
And just let *Love* take you-
When you-
Start Anew

A New Day Begins

Life is always changing-
And a new day begins.
Life has its challenges,
Its joys.
The good news is while
You're here there's always
The opportunity to live
Each day as if it's your last.
Take each experience
And always see the blessing
Behind every one.
Sometimes things don't always
Work out as we hope.
But never give up on *Hope.*
Sometimes the rain comes
To make room for the sun to shine
Even brighter.
For life is always changing-
And-
A New Day Begins!

Time Heals, And So Does Love

Time heals all wounds,
And so does *Love*.
Time gives us a better perspective,
A chance to see things differently.
For that can only be *Love*.

Always forgiveness releases
The hurt, the pain before.
For one's life doesn't always stay the same.
Things can change in minutes, hours, and years.
The good news is, there's always a chance
To change things each day of your life.

Yes, time heals all wounds.
But it's always the choices we make.
For as we invite the love to come within,
As we start to see the goodness in everyone.
We'll find that time not only heals-
And So Does Love.

You

Silence after the Storm,
The Storm that was raging
So long.
The Storm is over now.
Time to start a new direction.
Time to find a new sense of purpose.
Leaving what is familiar,
Even with new ventures to seek.
The old will not be again.
And taking it one step at a time,
It will be alright.
For I'm here,
Alive like I never been before.
Thank you Lord-
I begin here!
I begin with-
You!

Always There

You're always there though every trial,
Every triumph,
Your peace I find.
I lift my head up high,
Knowing my help comes from-
You.

I Praise You,
Every minute,
Every hour,
Every day.
For you're always there
Guiding me through it all.
Reassuring me so much.

You're my salvation,
My joy in the morning
To hold me as the evening comes,
And on to the next new day.

There's so much I can say about you.
Your goodness,
Your grace.
And I Thank you
To Know-
You're-
Always There.

Home

Balancing it all together,
What makes sense is the
Purpose of why I'm here.
Where I am meant to be-
At peace always,
In my soul always.
And yes,
Love I find everywhere.
While other things come and go,
Love never dies!
I see the morning sun,
I start a new day.
And it's all because of you.
You have given me new life.
Much greater than I can ever imagine.
It never left me.
Though at times I've moved away from it.
And this is where I will stay.
So glad I found my way back- *here.*
Dear Lord!
So glad I'm-
Home.

His Amazing Love

Sometimes what we pray for is not always what we need. And sometimes He doesn't always answer our prayers in the way we are expecting. But know that He does answer prayers always in His time. Faith is all about trusting in Him to know that He will supply all our needs.

All that He asks is that we place our trust in Him, Praising Him through the joyous times, and not so joyous of times. For as life shows us what is so amazing about His love, His mercy is that He blesses us through our joys and through our trials each and every time.

There's A Beautiful Voice Inside Of Me

There's a beautiful voice inside of me-
Instilling my faith in You.
And I thank you for every challenge –
Every *joy* in my life.

For with every challenge-
There's *A Blessing* every time.
And for every joy there's the reassurance –
You're always there with no doubt.

There's a beautiful voice inside of me,
That when things are not going well-
You give me the strength to see it through.
And more than ever *I Praise You* even more.

There's a beautiful voice inside of me,
That encourages me to go even further
Than I can ever have dreamed imaginable.
For all things are possible with you.

There's a beautiful voice inside of me-
Instilling my faith in You.
And Dear Lord!-
I thank you for every challenge –
Every joy in my life.
There's A Beautiful Voice Inside of Me!

In Due Season

When I think about all the blessings
He brings.
When I think about His Grace- His Love,
I can only stay where he wants me to be.
I cannot doubt Him,
No matter what,
No matter the challenges.
And when the storms come,
And it seems as though they will not pass,
I look up to Him to know
He's my help,
He's my friend.
And whatever my desires,
I know He will grant.
Yes,
Always-
In Due Season

Staying In Faith

Sometimes your dreams may seem
There're not being fulfilled.
But never lose sight of the purpose He has for you.
For as you believe with abiding faith-
He will give you the desires of your heart.

He has already blessed you through every trial-
Through every joy.
Always give Him the Praise through the joyous times.
And more so through your most difficult times.
For there's a reason for all things.

Nothing is impossible for Him.
For all things are possible no matter
How hopeless they may seem.
He will see you through any storm imaginable.

Hold on to your – *faith.*
He will get you to where you are to be.
Nothing is impossible for Him.
He has a purpose and design for your life.
Hold On To Your- Faith!

As I Plant The Seeds Of My Garden

As I Plant the Seeds of My Garden,
I plant my goals, my dreams,
And my visions of all I wish to do.
I cultivate the many goals,
I work towards to pursue.

As I Plant the Seeds of My Garden,
I vision my dreams blossoming with
Many opportunities.
And with self-determination,
My visions become a reality.

As I Plant the Seeds of My Garden,
I'm learning in accomplishing great
Achievements,
And Success,
Comes Courage,
And the belief in You!

I plant my goals,
My dreams,
And my visions.
Making them possible to become true.
As I Plant the Seeds of My Garden.

I Abide In You

You are the *joy* in the morning.
You are the *strength* I need each day.
You are the *wind* that holds me through every storm.

You are the *light* through the darkness.
You are the *sunshine* through the rain.
You are the *anchor* when the waters overflow.
And when *danger* is near,
Your arms surround me to know
You will never leave me.

For it's my *faith* that keeps me going.
It's my *trust* in you-
The reassurance,
The peace within my soul
That wherever I am-
Dear Lord!
I believe things that seem impossible
Are possible always-
With You!

Jesus My Friend Forever More

Let me tell you about my friend Jesus.
His *Love* is here today and *Always*.
He gives me a second chance,
A third chance,
A fourth chance to get it right.
He cares for me.

Let me tell you about my friend Jesus.
He has given me salvation like no other.
I can count on Him each and every time.
For His Mercy-
His Kindness-
His Compassion is so true.
He cares for me.

Let me tell you about my friend Jesus.
Who will never let you down.
When you need a friend to talk to
He listens,
He comforts you and holds your hand.
He cares for me.

Let me tell you about my friend Jesus.
For if you lose your way,
Do not worry-
Do not be afraid-
Just trust in Him.
And know that His Light is the reassurance -
He's a friend forever more.
Oh!- How He Cares for Me!

The Leap of Faith

Take the leap of *faith* and believe
Each step you take empowers you
To go the distance.
Find strength through each challenge
You so endure.
And when disappointments come,
Receive them as blessings
To keep going even more.
Never give up,
No matter what comes your way,
No matter how difficult the climb.
Just know as you keep going,
His Mercy,
His Love,
Will never fail you.
Take the Leap of Faith
And –*Believe.*

His Amazing Love

My Lord!-
You're my strength- my song.
You're the joy in the morning –
My healer of all my hurts- my pains-
You're my salvation.

For no matter what I go through.
For no matter what each day may bring-
You keep blessing me through it all.

My Lord!
You not only heal-
You're merciful-
And Yes!-
You're a fixer too!

For to trust in You I must.
With all my heart and soul-
I surrender it all.

My Lord!-
You're my strength- my song.
You're the joy in the morning-
My healer of all my hurts- my pains-
You're my salvation!
You keep blessing me through it all.
Oh! Your Amazing Love!

The Lord Watches Over Me

I do not fear the darkness at night.
For the sparrow stays within my sight.
Oh! How The Lord Watches Over Me.

I do not fear the arrows that come at me
During the day.
For the Lord is all around,
He is with me in every way.
The Lord Watches Over Me.

I do not dwell too long in despair.
For I know I am in the Lord's care.
The Lord He Watches Over Me.

I trust in the Lord, I hold on to his
Unchanging hand.
For when I am weak, He helps me stand.
The Lord Watches Over Me.

I will stay in the house of the Lord,
He will never leave me.
For I know with Faith,
He is with me through eternity.
Oh! How The Lord Watches Over Me.

This Day, A Dream,
A Promise Fulfilled

As we live our best life, to be all we can be, we enlighten our spirits to enormous possibilities beyond our imagination. One person's dream can inspire many to move for change. One person can make a difference, to stand behind the principles of life, liberty, and the pursuit of happiness that we all wish for, hope for, and live for.

There comes a time when a unique individual rises to the occasion in making a difference for the better. To stand tall in the midst of controversy, and with the Love of God to do what is right.

All About Honor

Honor is to live by truth, integrity,
And giving the best of yourself.
To stay true to the promise-
The commitment set forth-
Forever and always to do what is right.

Honor is never falling short of being honest
But never unkind.
Sometimes it's making sacrifices,
And letting go of things you desire to have
For the betterment of someone else.

Honor is standing tall when opposition
Is heavy upon you-
From every direction imaginable.
And yet as you keep the faith,
And believe in your heart doing the right thing,
Is what matters the most.

Honor is to live by truth, integrity,
And giving the best of your self.
For the true hero stays true to the promise-
The commitment set forth-
Forever and always to do what is Right.

Living To Purpose

Fulfillment comes through the passion
That lies deep within your heart.
Knowing your *purpose* and what God has
For your life-
Gives true meaning to why you're here.

For we all have a *purpose*-
We're all here for a reason.
And there's a reason for all things,
Throughout this vast and most beautiful world.

The most important thing is to never give up
On your passion-the gift He gives to you alone.
And always follow your passion no matter the distance,
No matter the challenges large or small.

Follow your passion no matter the obstacles along the way,
No matter what each moment of each day so brings
Through the trials and through the joys-
Just stay in *faith*.

Knowing your *purpose*
And what God has for your life-
Gives true meaning to why you're here.
For *true fulfillment* comes when you follow your passion -
That lies deep within your heart.

Walls

Walls divide us, separate us,
And keep us away.
Love has no place to stay.
Walls limit us to only go so far.
They stagnate us from being who we are.

Walls promote ignorance,
And encourage discrimination.
Differences are not welcomed,
Leaving not much room for communication.

Walls block understanding from coming in.
They breathe prejudice outwardly,
And within.

Walls keep our spirits dormant.
They do not allow us to trust.
They close hearts to where we don't give
The best of us.

Walls – Divide! Divide! Divide!
And behind them we hide.

Walls- For if we bring them down.
Love! Love! Love!
Will stay around.
Walls!

A Soldier For Peace

In memory of Dr. Martin Luther King Jr.

A Soldier for peace stands mighty and strong.
He stands against racial injustice,
With the love of God-
He Marches On!

A Soldier for peace fights for the civil rights
Of an oppressed people,
For justice and *"sweet liberty."*
A Soldier fights for their dignity,
For their place,
For equal opportunity.

He leads hundreds on sit-ins,
Protests,
Demonstrations for peace,
Fighting for their freedom,
Yours, and mine.
A Soldier for peace stands tall,
As he fights to end racial discrimination for all time.

A Soldier for peace was shot down.
But his fight for freedom and justice for all-
Remains Strong!
This Soldier For Peace-
A Mighty Warrior!
Brother Martin!
Your Memory Lives On!

Soldiers for peace light the candle of hope to burn brightly in the hearts of all.

A Pioneer's Journey

In fond memory of Coretta Scott King

You've traveled many roads for peace and humanity.
I admire your strength, your courage, your grace.
Thank you for continuing the dream for Martin.
Thank you for reminding us about tolerance and love.
Thank you for the fight for freedom, and freedom!
Thank you for staying strong through it all.
I wish I could have met you,
And I thank you for the brief time you were here.
Thank you for your beautiful spirit.
Thank you for impacting my life, and many others.
Thank you for your strength,
Your Courage,
Your Grace.
Thank you–
Dear Coretta

Choices

We can choose to be negative,
Or we can choose to be positive.
We can live in darkness,
Or we can turn on the light if we so choose.

We can choose to follow our dreams,
Or we can choose not to.
We can limit ourselves to go only so far,
Or we can seek our desires to endless possibilities
If we so choose.

We can make our own truth with
Jealousy, envy, and paranoia,
Or we can open our minds to the truth
If we so choose.

We can choose to be at war,
Or we can choose to be at peace.
We can harvest the seeds of ignorance and hate,
Or we can harvest the seeds of love if we so choose.

We choose the directions we take in our lives!
We choose the directions we take in our lives!
We Make Our Own-
Choices!

All Of A Sudden

Children will no longer be killing children.
All Of A Sudden

Families will spend more time together, not apart.
All Of A Sudden

People will start to talk and not argue.
All Of A Sudden

Police will serve and protect all their citizens,
No matter race or disability.
All Of A Sudden

There will be no more hunger in the land.
All Of A Sudden

There will be a cure for cancer and the sick will
Have hope.
All Of A Sudden

All of us will have a better quality of life.
All Of A Sudden

There will be no more hate- only love.
For before you know it-
God's Love will conquer all.
All Of A Sudden!

Where The Grass Is Green

There has to be a place- Where the Grass is Green,
Where Love is- always love.

There has to be a place- Where the Grass is Green,
Where I can be me,
And not concern myself if it's ok.

There has to be a place- Where the Grass is Green,
Where patience lies,
And positive energy spreads in every direction.

There has to be a place- Where the Grass is Green,
Where there's no fear to live each day,
And to trust is common practice.

There has to be a place- Where the Grass is Green,
Where the quality of life is abundant,
And working hard has more value.

There has to be a place – Where the Grass is Green,
Where war is just a distant memory of yesterday.
And peace is something we don't have to dream about.

There has to be a place- Where the Grass is Green,
Where Love keeps growing-
Crushing hate to the ground.

There has to be a place- Where the Grass is Green,
Where love is- always *Love*.
There has to be a place-
Where The Grass Is Green.

Inspiration

To believe all is possible,
That seems impossible,
To always encourage,
To enlighten the spirit,
To spread a little love wherever you go.
And just maybe as you pass it on,
The world will be more beautiful.
And before you know what a difference
You've made.
A more beautiful world you can ever
Have dreamed.
If you could only imagine
Such an inspiration that would be?

This Day, A Dream, A Promise Fulfilled

One's dream fulfills the hope of love and humanity for all
Dedication to Barack Obama The President of the United States

A dream has come this day,
Filled with hopes,
Opportunities,
To live our best life,
To be all we can be,
Explore all possibilities beyond our most imagination.
To discover our own uniqueness.
To open our minds,
To listen,
To hear with *Love*.

A dream has come this day,
With a leader whose voice speaks not only for self,
But for others as well.
Building a foundation
To Grow,
To Prosper,
To Achieve,
Dreams we all wish for ourselves.

A dream has come this day,
To fulfill the promise we can build a world
Of Hope,
Of Opportunity,
Of Tolerance,
Of Understanding-
And Love.

A dream has come this day,
For all to see and know.
Looking over the horizon,
A Dream, A Promise Fulfilled- *This Day.*

Sing A Song For Hope

As a New Year begins,
Let's sing a song for – *Hope*-
That the sorrows of yesterday's past
Will not be unnoticed.

As a New Year begins,
Let's hold on to *hope* for where we should go now-
To continue to stand for the injustices –
To change what is wrong- for all of us to be free.

As a New Year begins,
Let's hold on to *hope*-
That we will always be more tolerant of our differences,
Always letting the love inside of us shine.

As a New Year begins,
Let's hold on to *hope*-
That we can all make a difference- large or small-
Always with our hearts open wide.

As a New Year begins,
Let's- *Sing A Song For- Hope.*
We can make today and tomorrow brighter than yesterday.
We can make a difference- large or small.

As a New Year begins- May we come to *Love* one another.

Always Love

There's nothing more beautiful than love. You can have much faith that will move mountains. You can do the most noblest of things giving away your most valuable possessions. And you can succeed to the highest level in accomplishing great achievements. But without love, it holds no value.

Love never fails you, even when the world seems not kind. For when one person has love, it encourages others to come to know love. Love invites the heart to not be selfish, to give for just the sake of giving. Love is compassionate, tolerant, and kind. Love not only concerns itself with achieving, but always looks out for the well- being of others. Never give up on love. It's the only that last. There's nothing more beautiful than anything as- Love!

The Way of Love

As we hope for a brighter tomorrow.
May we see that even when the sun
Does not always shine each day as we awake,
That we can find- Love.

And may each of us discover
That love is always inside our hearts
Ready to shine, no matter what each day so brings.

For love is not measured by how much wealth
Or material value one may possess.
But more so by the love one gives from the heart open wide.

As we hope for a brighter tomorrow.
May His peace surround us always.
And may we come to know only
His Grace-
His –
Way of Love.

Hold On To Love

What brings us more together is- *Love.*
We can have many things to make our lives
Most comfortable.
We can climb the highest plateau-
Fulfill our dreams-
Give all that we own.

But what's most everlasting,
And more greater than we can ever have-
Is Love.

With *Love* we can always have hope
That each day will be brighter than yesterday.

And what we have now at this moment with *Love-*
We can live our dreams-
Be the best of ourselves.
And encourage others to know – *Love.*

Hold on to *Love!*
And let the *Love* shine inside of you.
Never doubt it.

For what brings us more together-
What's most everlasting,
And more greater than we can ever have-
Is Love!

Always Another Way

There's always another way in looking
At any given situation.
Sometimes what we may perceive
Is not always what's true.
But when we see with love-
We will never lose.

Sometimes we like to believe the worst.
And sometimes we like to convince ourselves
That what appears on the surface is true.
And before we know we set judgment
Making our own truth.
But when we see with love-
We'll never lose.

Sometimes we may rush judgment
About someone before we know the truth.
For as time passes most truths show themselves.
And when we set judgment are we kind.
But when we see with love-
We'll never lose.

There's always another way in looking
At any given situation.
For sometimes what we perceive
Is not always what's true.
But we'll never lose when we see with – *Love.*
There's- Always Another Way.

The Beauty Of Love

As you love, you live fulfilled.
And as you give love, you encourage
Others to give too.
But remember, there're times when love
May not be accepted or received by some.
And sometimes you may feel if it's worth the try.
But just stop and think
As you turn a negative situation
To a positive one,
You'll find much peace, much joy
You can ever imagine when you always
Answer to your heart.
Can you ever imagine anything greater?
For that's-
The Beauty of Love.

Love With Your Heart

When you find at those moments that the world is not kind-
Love with your heart.
For it's not always about how much people care-
But more so how much you care.

When you find that the love you give is never enough -
Love with your heart.
Forgive! Forgive! - As much as a thousand times over.

When you feel you do your best, and no one seems to notice-
Love with your heart.
For the real joy is always giving your very best.

When you find for one day more disappointments come.
Love with your heart.
Hold on to hope- stay true to your faith
And know that the sun will shine
Before you know.

Love with your heart when someone treats you unkind.
Wear a smile —never lose the joy inside of you.
Love with your heart when you feel persecution from others.
Pray and believe all things are possible with God's Mercy and Love.

Love with you heart through every trial – through every joy.
For He blesses you each and every day of your life.

Love with your heart and know that the Love you give -
Will also come back to you many times over-
When You Love With Your Heart.

May Each Day Lord I See You

Lord!-
May each day I see only you when trouble comes.
May each day I see only you when it seems no hope.
May each day I see only you
When the world is not at its best.
May each day I see only you
When sorrow is all around.

May each day I see your goodness
And grace shine throughout
As the morning comes,
As the noon day appears,
And as the evening makes its way
Before I lay down to sleep.

And Dear Lord!-
May your peace spread through every
River, ocean, mountain, hilltop,
And every shore -
For all to see and know.
Dear Lord!-
May Each Day I See You!

The Lord's Grace

There's nothing like the Lord's Grace.
A feeling within your soul-
A journey to the right place.

A feeling of negativity to no longer
Enter your mind.
True goodness, righteousness,
And always love you will find.

For no matter where you are,
His Love is always around.
And with His Love, it lifts you up in spirit,
You're heavenly bound.

It is a journey towards true salvation
For the rest of your days.
For the Lord's Grace is a feeling of *Love*-
In your heart always.
For there's nothing like-
The Lord's Grace

Always Love

Sometimes you may not see *Love* present.
And sometimes love seems as though
It doesn't stay around too long.
But when you find there's no Love around-
Hold on to it more than ever.
It's the only thing that- Last.

The world cannot live without Love-
And what's so amazing-
It never lets you down.
The more you invite love,
The more you share love-
Wonderful things happen!

Never give up on *Love*.
Hold on to it more than ever-
For it's the only thing that *–Last!*

Each Day I Awake

The world is most beautiful
When the sun shines on a-
Snow capped winter's morning.

The world is most beautiful
When spring is in full bloom-
Trees of Cherry Blossoms,
And gardens of flowers all around.

The world is most beautiful
When summer nights showcase the stars above-
No matter where you are.

The world is most beautiful
When autumn leaves keep falling
On those cool days just before winter.

And the world is most beautiful -
Each day I awake -
I still see *Love* no matter
Where I may be-
I see *Love* –
With the hope for an even brighter tomorrow-
Each Day I Awake.

Closing Poem

What Is A Christian Woman?

A Christian Woman praises the Lord
Through her trials, and through her joys.
She looks for the good in others.
She forgives a thousand times over.
She makes no list of wrongs.
She opens the door to understanding.
She listens and hears with love.
She finds peace through the suffering, and the pain.
She lives her days blessed.
She never forgets her family commitments.
She speaks truthfully her opinions with kindness,
And resolve.
She lives with compassion
No matter her circumstance.
She prays with a humble heart, without ceasing,
And always with Faith.
A Christian Woman is a doer,
And believer of the Word.
She's always giving of her heart.

Always give with your heart. For there's nothing more beautiful in all the world than- Love.

CPSIA information can be obtained
at www.ICGtesting.com
Printed in the USA
BVOW08s1916020217
475187BV00001B/50/P